Bedroom
makeovers

DISCARD

Frances Halliday

DISCARD

D1529956

B
BETTERWAY BOOKS
CINCINNATI, OHIO

LONDON PUBLIC LIBRARY
20 EAST FIRST STREET
LONDON, OHIO 43140

4/02

C o n t e n t s

The bedroom is often the last room in the home to be decorated. And yet it is the one room where you can really express yourself. In this book, the same bedroom has been given six makeovers using a variety of color schemes and painting styles to show you how different one room can look. Paint is inexpensive and offers an immediate way to update not only your walls but your floors, furniture, and accessories too. Today's demand for color has led to a huge growth in the range of paint colors available.

Color is a wonderful tool; it can literally transform everything it touches, and it is a vital part of our lives. It affects us in a way that we cannot fully appreciate: it can induce a range of feelings within us, and can cause us to respond in ways that we do not understand. Color can assist in making changes to our moods from happy to sad and from good to bad. Our unique ability to define differences in color separates and distinguishes us from all other species. With so many magazines dedicated to homes and interiors, paint manufacturers are producing more and more color ranges, giving us more color choices than ever before.

This book should be used as a practical guide to selecting paints and colors for your bedroom. Discussion on color theory will help you to choose and use color in the home. Practical advice on paint products and their suitability for different surfaces is combined with inspirational examples showing the use of color and its effect. The selection of projects undertaken here can all be adapted to suit your own particular ideas for your own bedroom.

The color schemes used in this book vary from fresh, bright lemon and lime to warm terra-cotta, and from moody blue to a riot of color in the Matisse-style bedroom. In addition to flat painting of walls and woodwork, several paint effects are introduced. If you have been discouraged in the past from attempting paint effects because of the complicated process involved with oil paint, acrylic paints, which are water based, will be a welcome discovery. They can be adapted very easily and are available from most home decorating stores. Water-based varnish was also used to create several of the room makeovers. The process of mixing small quantities of latex paint with water-based varnish is easy and allows you to experiment with different forms of application.

All the paint effects and techniques shown throughout this book can be used in many different colors and styles. Experiment first and try out your ideas on lining paper or

pieces of wood. Keep these in your bedroom for a few days and see how they change throughout the day in the different light levels.

In these makeovers color is not only enjoyed in paint but also in other elements such as fabric and wallpaper. The individual projects allow as much or as little of that particular look to be re-created. With information on preparation and basic techniques, an absolute beginner in home decoration can have the confidence to put these ideas into practice. Everything you need to know to get started is contained within these projects.

Use these color schemes and project ideas to give your bedroom a new lease on life; after all, there is no excuse for putting up with decor you don't like. And an advantage of experimenting with paint and color is that if you don't like the finished result, you can re-paint the surface and start again. The tremendous sense of achievement you have when looking at the end result is very pleasurable.

Using color in your bedroom

Color is one of the most wonderful and versatile tools of interior decoration. With the use of paint you can transform the darkest room into a light, bright space, or the loudest decor into a muted paradise of sophistication. Knowing how to mix and use color is crucial to the success of any interior. However, because color is essentially an abstract concept, many people find it difficult and bewildering to fathom. This lack of confidence is largely due to an ignorance of the basic principles of color. In color theory, as with most things, there are certain rules and guidelines that should be followed. As your confidence grows, you can even try to break a few.

THE COLOR WHEEL

The color wheel is one of the most important ways to understand color. It is a simplified version of the spectrum: circular in shape, it is an arrangement of the primary colors of red, yellow, and blue, and the secondary colors of orange, green, and violet. From these colors all

Color can be used to change the shape and size of a room. Rich, strong colors like crimson diminish the space and create a warm, dramatic environment. Cool blue creates an airy quality that can be accentuated by the use of accessories in contrasting colors. Soft pastel colors blend together for a calming environment. Color can also be applied to a divided space for interest.

other colors are made, including grays, browns, and neutrals.

Primary colors are equidistant on the color wheel. A primary color cannot be made by mixing any other colors. These primary colors can be mixed together in varying proportions to produce every other color in the spectrum. When two primary colors are mixed together in equal quantities they produce a secondary color, for example, when blue and yellow are mixed they create green; when yellow and red are mixed they create orange; while when red and blue are mixed they produce violet.

A tertiary color is made by mixing an equal amount of a primary color with the secondary color next to it on the color wheel. By adjusting the proportions of the primary or secondary colors you can create a wide range of subtle colors.

There are two basic ways in which colors react with one another: they will either harmonize or contrast. This is easy to see on the color wheel: colors that harmonize are close to each other while those that contrast are placed far apart. If you wish to use colors that harmonize, choose a section of the color wheel and work with just those colors that are adjacent to one another, for example blue with blue-green or blue with blue-violet.

The colors situated opposite one another on the color wheel are known as complementary colors. There are three main sets of complementary colors: red and green, blue and orange, and yellow and violet. When two colors of the same tone and intensity are used in a room they will intensify each other, causing the eye to jump rapidly from one color to the other, thus giving a shimmering effect. When opposite colors meet they create impact. They enhance each other and produce a vibrant visual sensation; each color will appear brighter against its neighbor than it would alone. For example, green and red can work well together in a room when used in the right proportions; equal amounts of each color can result in a jarring shimmering effect, but small hints of red in a predominantly green room can be very exciting. It is sometimes better to use near or split complementaries, for example, turquoise and pink, as used in the Matisse room (see page 78). In this room, highlights of red, green, purple and orange were used in the accessories to emulate the busy vitality of a Matisse painting.

The use of one warm color alongside a cool one helps to create a feeling of balance within a room. Colors are either warm or cool. The warm colors are those that fall within the yellow-orange-red sections of the color wheel whereas the cool colors range through the purple-blue-green segments.

COLOR AND MOOD

One of the most important aspects of color is that it is emotive; it stimulates all the senses, not just the eyes. Color can be used to suggest and to accentuate the mood of a room as well as create an emotional response from the viewer. It can trigger a flow of images, emotions, and sounds. Blue makes us think of sky and sea, mountains, and streams. Depending on the color and tone used, it can denote freshness and lightness or melancholy and alienation. Yellow is the color that conjures up images of sun and flowers, but it can also be harsh and acidic. It is therefore

vital that the correct color and tone be chosen.

TONAL VALUE

When choosing a color, it is important to consider the depth of tone you desire. The tonal value of any color will change with the effect of light. The more a surface faces away from the source of light the darker it will become. The framework of light and dark

The color wheel below shows a simplified version of the spectrum with the primary colors of red, yellow, and blue, and the secondary colors of orange, green, and violet. From these colors all other colors are made.

B R I G H T

PINK

Pink is an extraordinary color. It can range from pale cotton candy, through sugar-almond pink to subtle salmon. Pink works well with turquoise, its complementary color, and with the colors on either side of it on the color wheel, violet and red. Psychologists believe that to sleep in a pink room will leave you in a good, optimistic frame of mind.

areas that make up a room is often what initially attracts attention and will give an immediate introduction to the mood or atmosphere of a room. Tones and colors are modified by adjoining colors; a color that appears dark when next to a white wall may well seem to have a lighter tone when surrounded by other colors. Colors and tones should never be regarded in isolation, but in terms of how they relate to others around them. All colors and tones are influenced by neighboring ones. When two colors are viewed side by side, the contrast between them is enhanced. Each touch of color added to the room alters the relationship of the colors that are already there.

C O L O R   H A R M O N Y

Harmony is possibly the most subtle and evocative of all reactions between colors and can be used with great effect to create mood in a room. While contrast is dramatic and may emphasize a special feature or area of the room, harmony is gentle and easy on the eye. There is harmony between those hues that lie on the same section of the spectrum or color wheel; for example, between the yellow and green featured in the lemon and lime room (see page 38). This is a combination frequently found in nature in the harmony of a spring landscape. Although harmonious schemes are often the most pleasing and easy to achieve, the very qualities they possess that make them harmonious may also make them monotonous. So it is important to enliven the color scheme with suggestions of complementary color.

CHOOSING COLORS

At an early age peer pressure can influence color choice. For example, we are taught from an early age to see red for danger, black for sadness, white for innocence, pink for a girl, and blue for a boy. Similarly, adults' color preferences can be dramatically controlled by rules of conformity, society, and by individual experiences.

Like everything else, paint colors are subject to fashion fads. Just as clothes designers change their color range each year, so do the fabric and wallpaper design houses. This puts pressure on paint manufacturers to keep up with current trends. Thus, each year, more and more subtler shades are added to paint ranges. Consumers can only benefit from the wider choice, but it does make the task of choosing colors all the harder.

There are some color combinations, however, that never seem to fall prey to fashion, and these go on evolving through the years, still managing to look new and exciting; blue and yellow, or the classic neutral range are

SOOTHING
AQUA

Aqua is a color derived by the mixing together of blue and green. It is on the cooler side of the color wheel, which means that it recedes in a room, creating the feeling of space and depth. Aqua is a versatile color with a gentle, cleansing ambience and, with its connotations of water, it creates a soothing atmosphere, perfect for the bedroom.

A P P L E

GREEN

Green is a good natural color, varying in hue from citrus lime to sage, and is found on the cool side of the color wheel. It can look dramatic when partnered by red or by orange. For a more harmonious combination, use blue and yellow. Green also works well with the pale natural range, like vanilla and linen.

obvious examples. But for some, the idea of using a color that has been used before is not appealing; the yearning for originality and inspiration is too strong to suppress.

EFFECT OF LIGHTING

Before choosing colors for your bedroom, check the quality of natural light your room receives. In sunlight, colors usually take a stronger or deeper tone than in poor natural light. In a bedroom that has poor natural light you might do well to choose pale colors for your decorating scheme, which will reflect light back into the room rather than absorb it. It is also important to determine the general direction from which the light is entering the room, as this may alter at different times of the day. A room that faces due south and so is a little dull in the mornings might induce you to brighten it up by painting the walls a sunny yellow; this could send you racing for your sunglasses in the afternoon when the room is flooded in natural sunlight. One solution is to opt for colors and tones that work well in both artificial and natural light.

CREATING ATMOSPHERE

Another aspect to consider is the atmosphere you want to create in your bedroom. Dark and warm colors can make a room cosy and more intimate, but they can also make the room appear smaller. Red, orange, yellow, and pink are generally described as advancing colors; that is, they appear to come toward you when applied to the wall. Warm colors are good to use in cool, north-facing rooms, as they provide a feeling of warmth and create cosy interiors. Light, cool colors, on the other hand, can create a feeling of space and airiness in a room. Blue, white, and green are cool colors; use them in a south-facing room to create a fresh, calm scheme.

All the room makeovers featured in this book have a strong individual atmosphere that was purposely created by the careful use of color, furnishings, and accessories. In the terra-cotta room, for example, the atmosphere derived from the memory of a Greek holiday. In the Matisse room, a painting dictated the use of sunny colors and roughly painted walls.

Atmosphere is dependent not just on color but on texture as well. When choosing paint, there are many options available in addition to latex: semigloss, gloss, eggshell, and satin are all now available in acrylic water-based paint, as well as in oil paint. With the introduction of water-based varnish, glazes can be mixed up easily; these give an extra dimension of texture to a room when applied over plain white walls.

TRANQUIL

BLUE

True moody blue is a timeless favorite. It is the supreme cool color, evoking a sense of tranquillity. Blue's rich and varied tones are endless. Deep, intense blues can give an energetic and fresh feel to a room, adding depth and contrast. Pale, subtle, and muted shades of blue can create the feel of open, airy spaces.

SUNSHINE
YELLOW

Yellow is the most cheerful of all colors. Its bright, light-reflecting quality cannot help but lift your spirits. Yellow is warm and will bring a source of light to even the darkest of rooms. Its tonal range travels from citrus lemon through to sultry yellow ocher, with sunny and muted shades in between. Yellow works well with blue, purple, and green.

TESTING COLORS

It is a good idea to do as much research as you can before commencing your decorating. If you intend to use a fabric for either blinds or curtains, then your color choice should reflect that. Perhaps this could be your starting point or color reference. Always take a small piece of your chosen fabric or wallpaper with you when choosing either paint or accessories; don't rely on your memory, as it will undoubtedly let you down. Try to access as many of the design houses as you can. Treat yourself to a few of the interior magazines readily available at newsdealers. And when you feel that you have seen as much as you need to, go to your nearest paint supplier and collect a range of paint chips. Don't be afraid to take as many different tones of your color choice away with you as you like—they are there specifically for that purpose. Invariably the tones of color will change when you come to use it in your own environment. Color changes when it is compared with and against its opposite. For example, green will look far greener when next to the redder tones. Blue will look bluer when it is next to pink, as they harmonize together.

Try out a few of your chosen paint effects on sheets of lining paper. This will give you a realistic sense of the color and the opportunity of perfecting the paint effect you are going to achieve. You can then pin these up in your bedroom and live with them for a while, observing how light changes the color at different times. Sometimes it is not the immediate impact that you desire; alternatively, the subtler effect may merge too far into the background when lived with for a time. This will also offer you the opportunity to see how the light changes throughout the day. This may take time and will require patience, but it will help to create the look that is right for you.

EXISTING FURNITURE

Very few people are in the happy position of starting from scratch with an unlimited budget and no commitments to a few inherited heirlooms or granny's rosewood wardrobe. If you do have to work around inherited objects, do this in a positive way and make the room work around them. Perhaps you could use a color indicated in a chair covering as the basis of your decorating scheme. If you really feel the need to change your decor and these items simply do not fit into the new color scheme, there is always the possibility of reupholstering, stripping or painting the pieces to match your room. Whatever you decide, don't ignore these items in your color scheme and pretend that they do not belong in your room, as the result will be one of incoherence and disappointment.

CALMING

LAVENDER

This beautiful atmospheric color sits on the color wheel between the two primary colors of blue and red. Because of the mix of warm and cool tones, there is a great balance within lavender's shade. You can either create a warm, pinky lavender, or a violet tone, which will recede. Use it with green, pink, or orange.

By applying the paint to both walls and wardrobe doors the spatial quality of the blue paint effect is enhanced. The use of white highlights on the picture rail and accessories offers a clean fresh contrast.

Paint Products

The selection of paints, varnishes, and other products for decorating that are available can be confusing for an enthusiastic amateur. These pages will help you through the maze of products and guide you to the correct selection for the project you are undertaking and the surfaces on which you intend to apply it.

Paint is colored pigment suspended in a medium that makes it spreadable and gives it an acceptable drying time. Paint also contains the relevant chemicals to ensure that it does not rub off easily and that the color will not fade too much. It can be helpful to understand how paint is manufactured. There are two main processes involved: one for water-based paints and one for oil-based paints.

WATER-BASED PAINTS

Water-based paints are known as latex paints. They are water soluble and are made by pushing ground pigment (color in its purest form) into a solution of water and polyvinyl acetate (PVA) resin. PVA is a type of plastic. The pigment is forced into the resin and water at such high speed that it breaks up and disperses evenly. When you apply a PVA paint to your walls you are effectively applying a skin of colored plastic and water. The water evaporates and you are left with an even coating of colored plastic. The greater the shine on the PVA paint, the higher the ratio of plastic to water.

OIL-BASED PAINTS

Oil-based paints, such as eggshell and gloss, are more complicated to make and as a result are more expensive to buy. You can expect oil-based paints to last much longer than many water-based ones. Oil-based paint is made by first making a "binder," which is a mixture of linseed oil, acid, and alcohol. To this are added some thinners (mineral spirits) and ground white pigment, and this is then mixed. The pigment does not break up and disperse during this process so the mixture is then ground in a mill to ensure that an evenly whitened paint base results. Finally, more thinners are added, along with a chemical drier and some stainers. The product goes through a staining process before it is officially called paint. You may be familiar with paint base; this is the product to which the home decorating stores add stainers to color the paint to your requirements. So, when you apply oil-based paint you are simply covering your surface with colored oils. As it contains all these chemicals, it smells strong.

PRIMER

Primer can be either water or oil based. It is used on bare wood to seal the surface and keep the wood from swelling when the undercoat and top coat are applied.

UNDERCOAT

Undercoat can be either water or oil based. It is a thin surface preparation and is used to seal walls and woodwork before the top coat. It has a matte finish.

LATEX FLAT PAINT

Latex flat paint is practical and inexpensive to use for covering large areas quickly. As it is water based, it does not have an offensive smell and has no shine at all. Latex paints are difficult to wash if they become dirty but can be touched up very quickly and easily.

LATEX SATIN PAINT

Latex satin paint is much the same as latex flat paint but easier to clean if it gets dirty and has a slight shine to it. For creating paint techniques your base coat must have a slight shine, so this type of paint is recommended in place of flat finishes. There are now some washable latex paints on the market that help to overcome the difficulties of keeping a flat-painted surface looking like new.

EGGSHELL PAINT

Oil-based or eggshell paint has a definite satin shine to it and usually a greater intensity and luster of color. It is more expensive than latex paint but will last at least twice as long. Eggshell paint has an offensive smell and it is recommended that, when using it, you work in a well-ventilated area to prevent inhalation of the fumes. Eggshell paint takes longer to dry than water-based paints. However, the effect of oil-based paint on a surface is more professional than water-based paint.

GLOSS PAINT

Gloss paint is almost always oil based and has a full gleam to it. It is difficult to apply and should be brushed over a surface in two or three thin coats using a good-quality brush. Over time, the shine of the gloss will reduce and it will need repainting.

RADIATOR PAINT

Radiator paint has a lower quantity of ingredients that may yellow with heat. It also contains ingredients that keeps the paint from peeling off a hot surface or softening when the radiators are on. Radiator paint is much more expensive to buy than other paints and the choice of colors is limited. If you are prepared to repaint your radiators as time goes by, then you can use any shade of eggshell paint. Always work on a cold surface.

TILE PRIMERS

Tile primers are designed for those who cannot afford the luxury of new tiles when changing the room decor. You can safely and effectively paint over your old tiles for a new look. Apply tile primer in two coats, leaving at least 16 hours between each coat as it dries very slowly. When the primer is dry, you can paint the tiles in any color you choose, using an eggshell paint for a long life.

UNIVERSAL STAINERS

These are colored stains in liquid form that can be added to water-based or oil-based paints to adjust the color. They are available in traditional artist's colors. Try raw umber for "dirtying" a color. Avoid black unless you are seeking a graying effect; it can be too artificial.

VARNISH

Varnish is just like paint but clear. Most varnish comes through the initial production stages as clear gloss. Silicon powders are added to make a satin or flat finish. Since these powders settle in the can, it is imperative to stir the varnish well before and regularly during use. Varnishes that claim to bring out the beauty of your wood may have some yellow colorants added to them. You can stain varnish very easily for your own use by stirring in some artist's colors. Use oil colors for polyurethane varnishes and acrylics for water-based varnishes.

Generally, the thinner the varnish, the easier it is to apply and the better will be the quality of your finished work. Before buying varnish, shake the cans and choose the ones in which the contents sound most like water. Very thick varnishes, such as yacht varnish, look good after only a couple of coats, but the coats are very difficult and time consuming to apply. It is preferable to apply four or five coats of a thinner varnish for a smooth finish.

WOOD STAIN

Woodstain is most often used for coloring untreated or bare wood. It can be either water or spirit based. Wood stain soaks deep into the grain of the wood but is transparent so that the original grain will still show through. Apply the wood stain in generous quantities and wipe the surface with a soft cloth when dry. Wood stain does not actually protect raw wood and therefore you must apply a coat of varnish or wax over the surface after coloring it for protection.

WAX

Wax offers an easy way to bring some protection and sheen to wood. Wax will nourish and protect most wooden surfaces and can be repaired and touched up easily. Beeswax is still one of the best wood polishes (and also smells very pleasant). All you need to do is apply the wax just like a floor polish, let it dry, and then buff with a soft cloth. Reapply wax on a surface from time to time as the sheen dulls.

Waxes containing colorants are also available; these will stain the wood as you go. You may need to carry out several applications of colored wax before you achieve the color shown on the can. For the initial treatment of wood with wax you may benefit from hiring a professional buffer, such as those used to polish cars.

GLAZE

Glaze is another medium that can be colored for use in creating special paint effects such as ragging and dragging. In simple terms it makes the color slippery and movable. The glaze is applied with a paintbrush or roller and then, while it is still wet, it is manipulated with brushes, rags, plastic, or anything you like. When the effect is achieved, the glaze is allowed to dry. The paint effect will last as long as ordinary paints.

Glaze is available in oil- or water-based forms; the oil-based glaze has more luster and depth to it. When using glaze, take care to complete an entire section in one rapid session as, if the glaze begins to dry at the edges, you will see a significant "watermark" where the overlaps are. Stop in corners only, having brought the glazed section to a neat finish.

ENAMEL AND CRAFT PAINTS

These paints are sold in small quantities and are useful for small jobs, detailing, and murals. Their colors are very intense. Most enamels do not need to be protected with varnish and will keep their color for years. Craft paints, on the other hand, may be water based and might resist a surface which has been prepared in oils. Always buy the best craft paint you can afford. The color in cheap craft paint can fade rapidly.

ARTIST'S OIL CRAYONS

These crayons are just like children's wax crayons except that they are oil based. They can be used for touch-up jobs and for drawing fine lines where a paintbrush may be too bold, heavy, or difficult to handle. An oil crayon can be sharpened to a point just like a pencil, and the color can also be thinned or smudged with the aid of mineral spirits.

PURE PIGMENT

Sold in powder form by art supply stores, pure pigment is the base of all the traditional colors on an artist's palette. The color of pure pigment is the most intense available and it can be mixed into either oil- or water-based products. It is expensive, but you only need a small amount as you will not use that much at a time.

LINSEED OIL

Linseed oil can be used to make your own transparent paints by mixing with artist's oils or pure pigments, a dash of mineral spirits, and, very importantly, a few drops of driers. Use refined or boiled linseed oil to minimize the yellowing effect. Linseed oil does not dry without chemical help from driers.

DRIERS

These chemical additives can be added to oil paints to speed up the drying time. Be careful not to add too much; one teaspoon is sufficient for 32 fl oz (1 liter) of oil-based paint. Any more than this may affect the shine of the paint and make it appear powdery. Driers are an essential part of any painter's kit.

WHITING

A white powder, made from chalk, that can be added to homemade linseed oil paint in order to make it less transparent. Mix the oil into the powder a little at a time to avoid lumps, rather than putting powder into the paint. Whiting can also be used to make ready-made paints go further, but will have a slight whitening effect. Thin with turpentine, mineral spirits, or water, depending on the medium of your paint.

Troubleshooting

THE COLOR IS WRONG

If you are not happy with the color you have applied, you could re-paint the room. Alternatively, if the color you have applied is fairly pale or light, consider glazing over it using a simple paint technique such as color-washing or ragging. Your base color will be toned down by doing this but will still glow through the transparent glaze.

If the color looks too dark you could try sponging one or two lighter colors on top. Your base color will show through but the whole effect will become lighter and mottled. If you are using two or more colors for sponging, use the lightest color last.

THE SHEEN IS WRONG

If the paint you have used either does not have as much shine as you would like or is too shiny, there is a solution.

Buy some latex glaze with a gloss, eggshell, or flat finish, whichever is required, and apply a single coat of this on the dry paint surface. Latex glaze looks like milk when wet but dries clear.

THE PAINT IS WAXY

Careful preparation can often keep oil-based paint from drying or make it dry with a waxy feel. If you are painting on a wooden surface you must first prime the surface. Primers provide not only a smooth surface on which to paint but also a base on which the top color will dry and cure fully. If you have overlooked priming the surface, wash the troubled paint away with plenty of mineral spirits and steel wool and start on a primed surface.

If the paint is drying very slowly with a waxy feel to it then you have probably applied the coats too thickly. The surface of the paint is beginning to dry and cure and is sealing in the moisture underneath it. If you can, let the paint alone for a week and see if it dries. If the paint does not dry, scrape it off, wash the wood with mineral spirits and steel wool, and start again.

THE PRIMER IS NOT DRYING

This is a rare problem and is usually caused by the primer having been applied too thickly. Primer should be thin and soak into the new wood when applied, providing a smooth and even surface on which to apply the top color. If the room in which you are working is damp you may also encounter problems with drying. Try heating the room with a dry heat and see if the primer dries. If it still does not dry, scrape off the offending primer and begin again.

PAINT HAS BEEN SPILLED

Every painter's nightmare is to spill paint on the carpet. If the paint spill is small, let it dry without touching it at all. It can then be removed from the carpet pile with sandpaper. Water-based paint spills can be removed immediately by washing the area with plenty of water and blotting with clean rags. Larger oil-based spills will have to be washed with mineral spirits and then with soapy water. Before washing out a spill, remove all the paint you can by scraping from the outside of the spill inward.

NOT ENOUGH PAINT

If you notice the potential disaster of your paint running out in good time, you can stretch your paint by diluting it a little with the appropriate thinner and by making sure that you use every drop of the paint in which you have soaked your rollers and brushes rather than washing it away into the sink. Sometimes you can buy a small tester pot of latex paint to help with that last small area. If you are working with a color that you mixed yourself, and that cannot be repeated, then one wall or section of your room will have to be painted in a harmonizing shade or color.

SAGGING

The paint has been applied too thickly or each coat has not been allowed to dry fully before the next was applied. To deal with sagging paint you must first allow it to dry fully and then rub the offending areas down with wet-and-dry sandpaper (use it wet for best results) until it is perfectly smooth. Now paint the rubbed-down parts again using the same number of coats you used on the whole area.

POOR FLOW LEVEL

The effect pictured above is caused by poor flow level, which means that the paint is resisting the surface on which it is being applied. It usually occurs when water-based paint, such as latex, is being applied on an oil-based paint. For large areas you will be forced to buy new paint in oil-based form. For smaller areas, try washing the surface with detergent and a light scouring pad to remove any grease that may be sitting on the surface. If the paint still resists, you will have to resort to using oil-based paint.

CRACKING

Cracking is caused when paint or varnish is applied over a base layer of paint or varnish of different elasticity before it has been given long enough to cure (which can take up to a month). For example, two separate brands of varnish may react with each other and form cracks. To deal with cracking you must allow the surface to dry fully and then rub it down to make it ready for repainting. You could, however, consider leaving the cracking visible. It is a very popular aging technique, and many people seek this particular decorative effect.

DRIPS

Drips or "nibs" in the dried paint surface are usually simply oversights. Rub the dried drip away with fine sandpaper and re-paint the area. On high-gloss finishes you may need to apply a final coat over the entire area to disguise the patch where you rubbed away a drip.

Product	Quality	Thinners and brush cleaning	Use for	Apply with
Primer	Preparation for bare wood. Keeps wood from swelling	Turpentine or water (check the can)	Bare wood	Brush or small roller
Undercoat	Matte finish, thin surface preparation and sealer	Water or turpentine (check the can)	Walls, woodwork	Brush
Latex flat	No shine, general-purpose coverage	Water	Walls, new plaster	Large brush or roller
Latex satin	Satin sheen, general-purpose coverage	Water	Walls, murals, base for glaze work. Not for new plaster	Large brush or roller
Eggshell	Satin sheen, general-purpose coverage	Mineral spirits or turpentine	Walls, woodwork, and metal	Large brush or roller
Gloss	High shine, durable	Turpentine or water (check the can)	Woodwork, doors	Good-quality brush
Wood stain	Color without varnish for bare wood	Water or mineral spirits	Bare or unvarnished wood	Lint-free cloth or brush
Varnish— polyurethane	Oil-based wood and paintwork protection. Choice of shine	Mineral spirits or turpentine	Wood and to protect paintwork	Good-quality brush
Varnish— water-based	Fast-drying protection for wood and paintwork. Choice of sheen. Nonyellowing	Water	Wood and to protect paintwork	Brush or roller

Number of coats	Washable?	Area per quart (liter) in square yards (meters)	Notes	Drying time pre recoating	Drying time final coat	Undercoat
1	N/A	13 yards (12 meters)	Thin to a watery consistency. Rub down with sandpaper when dry	2–4 hours	N/A	No
1	N/A	13 yards (12 meters)	Stir well. Rub down with sandpaper when dry	Oil based— 8 hours. Water based— 2 hours	N/A	N/A
2	No	11 yards (10 meters)	Do not stir and avoid frost	1–2 hours	8 hours	No, but dilute first coat for raw wood
2	Yes, soapy water. Do not scrub	11 yards (10 meters)	Dark colours require 3 or more coats	1–2 hours	8 hours	Latex flat
2	Yes, household cleaners. Avoid ammonia	16 yards (15 meters)	Stir well before and during use	8 hours	24 hours	Primer or commercial undercoat
2	Yes, household cleaners. Avoid ammonia	13 yards (12 meters)	Slow to apply—use good-quality bristle brush. Oil based is more long wearing	4–8 hours	24 hours	Primer
1 or 2	No	8 yards (8 meters)	Apply generously with brush or cloth. When dry, wipe off excess with dry cloth. Stainers do not protect wood; always wax or varnish when dry	1–3 hours	1–3 hours	No
Up to 8	Yes, soapy water	11 yards (10 meters)	Use thinned and apply several coats for the greatest luster. May yellow as coats build up	4 hours	24 hours	No
Up to 8	Yes, but do not scrub	11 yards (10 meters)	Difficult to apply as evenly as polyurethane varnishes. Not as durable but fast drying and crystal clear. Do not use on oil-based paints	1 hour	8 hours	No

23

Product	Quality	Thinners and brush cleaning	Use for	Apply with
Wax	Protection and shine for wood	N/A	Bare or stained wood	Lint-free cloth
Oil-based glaze	Transparent	Mineral spirits or turpentine	Mix with artist's oils to make colored glaze for various paint finishes	Brush or roller
Craft paint	Intense colors for detailing and small areas	Various	Small craft projects	Soft brush
Artist's oil crayons and pastels	Intense, pure colors in stick form	Oil or turpentine	Detailing and drawing on walls, furniture, or paper	N/A
Pigment	Intense colors	Water	Make homemade paints for color-washing	Brush or roller
Car spray paint	Low or high sheen, durable, wide color range	Cellulose thinners	Stencils and basic coverage	Spray from the can
Glass paint	Transparent or matte	Acetone	Painting glass of all kinds. Transparent detail work	Soft artist's brush
Blackboard paint	Matte black, very opaque	Denatured alcohol	Interior matte finishes, blackboards	Brush
PVA glue	General-purpose sealer	Water	Walls or woodwork to seal or stick	Brush

Number of coats	Washable?	Area per quart (liter) in square yards (meters)	Notes	Drying time pre recoating	Drying time final coat	Undercoat
3	Yes, with more wax or soapy water	8 yards (8 meters)	Apply just like shoe polish, buff with a soft cloth between coats. Pure beeswax best for new wood; rewax often	3 hours	N/A	Wood stain (optional)
1 or 2	No	Depends on consistency	Good workability for ½ hour. Cheap way to extend color	6 hours	N/A	Oil-based eggshell base
1 or 2	Yes, do not scrub	N/A	Better quality than poster paints. Widely available in small quantities	½ hour	N/A	N/A
N/A	No	N/A	Allow to dry for 3 weeks or more before varnishing	N/A	N/A	N/A
1	Yes	N/A	Can be mixed with oil- or water-based products	N/A	N/A	N/A
1 or 2	Yes	N/A	Extremely hardwearing; wear a mask when spraying	1 hour	10 hours	Spray undercoat
1	Yes, do not scrub; check label	N/A	Brushstrokes always show up; beautiful vivid color selection	1 hour	4 hours	No
1 or 2	Yes, water only	11 yards (10 meters)	Fast drying, easy to repair and patch up	1 hour	4 hours	No
1	Yes, soapy water	13 yards (12 meters)	Dilute 1:1 with water. Apply with brush	1–2 hours	N/A	No

25

MAKEOVER PROJECT

Pastel Shades

These subtle pastel shades of raspberry pink, blue, lilac, vanilla, and mint green complement one another beautifully and the combination of them is deliciously inspiring. The harmonious blend of light and air creates a peaceful and relaxed space.

There is a huge variety of ice cream colors to choose from for your room scheme. As these pastel colors have the same creamy and chalky hue, it is possible to use a large number of them in the same room. This is normally inadvisable as one color can react against another, giving an

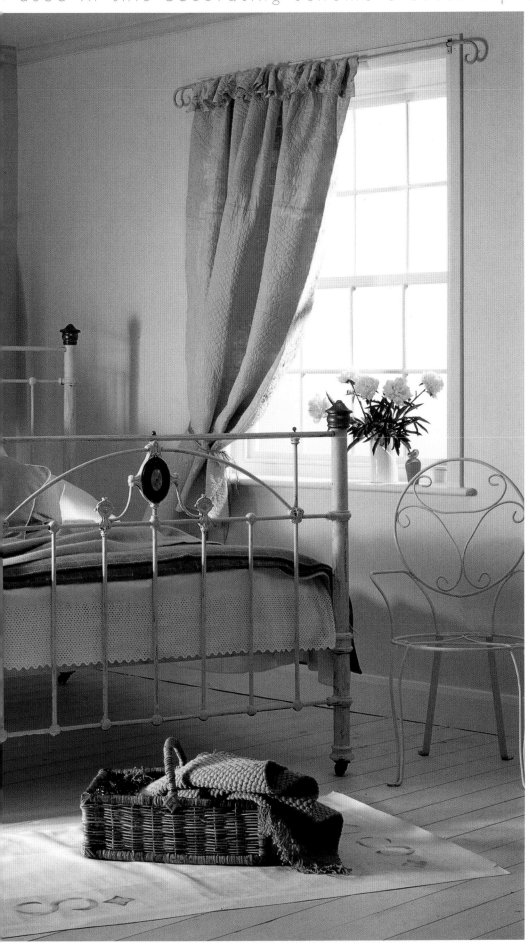

PROJECTS FROM THIS
MAKEOVER SHOW YOU

- HOW TO DRY-BRUSH A
  WALL

- HOW TO STENCIL A RUG

- HOW TO REVAMP AN
  IRON BED FRAME

- HOW TO MAKE A
  BEDSPREAD CURTAIN
  AND TIEBACK

overall inconsistency; however, in this case, the tonal range blends and shimmers together, with no one color dominating, and each color adding to the other's natural vibrance. The balance between warm and cool colors is broken only by the addition of accessories in slightly deeper tones; the furniture painted in a soft mid tone of lilac reaffirms the importance of color equality. When using more than one color in a room, give each color the same amount of space. To create a balanced feel to the color, you must use colors of similar intensity. The lack of pattern in the room helps to maintain the clean, uncluttered feel.

PREPARATION

Make sure that all holes in the ceiling or walls are filled with general all-purpose filler, and that any loose wallpaper is stuck down fast with wallpaper paste. Any slight indentations will show up more after the surface is decorated. Protect any furnishings that cannot be removed with dust sheets; cover the floor, too, as splashes and drips will inevitably land there.

Mix the glazes, making sure that you have the amount required. You will need a clean mixing pail, water-based varnish, and a small quantity of the paint in the color you want to apply. For each color glaze you will need 1 part latex paint to 2 parts water-based varnish. You can mix the glaze with a spatula; if, however, the quantity you require is great, use a paint paddle attached to an electric drill, to make mixing easier. Before applying glaze, mask off any adjoining surfaces with low-tack masking tape, as this will help to create clean lines.

DRY-BRUSHING

This technique is easy-to-achieve and results in a subtle broken paint effect that is perfect for pale paint colors, and also more suitable for this room scheme than a flat coat of latex paint.

EXPERT TIP
• *If the paint starts to flake when drying, it probably means that you have painted latex paint over an oil-based paint, such as gloss or distemper (see page 21 for the way to remedy this). Before painting with either acrylic or latex paint, always prepare the surface by rubbing it down with sandpaper and applying a good coat of all-purpose water-based primer.*

1 Using an all-purpose brush, apply a coat of vanilla latex paint over the surface to cover it entirely. Allow to dry.

2 Wrap sandpaper around a block of wood and use this to rub over the painted surface. This smooths the surface in readiness for the top coat of paint.

3 Mix up a glaze with 1 part pink latex to 2 parts water-based varnish. Dip an all-purpose brush in the glaze, then brush it over the surface in long vertical strokes. This effect allows the brushstrokes and part of the base coat to remain visible. Allow to dry.

MATERIALS

canvas rug

low-tack masking
tape

latex paint: pink,
aqua

water-based varnish

sponge

thick paper

craft knife

cutting mat

gray spray paint

stencil brush

gold paint

Stenciling a rug

Painted floors can offer a great opportunity to match exactly the color you are using on the walls, but they can be a little stark. Painting a rug in the same colors as the room softens the effect of the floor and unifies the room's color scheme. This rug not only introduces the aqua used on the walls at floor level but also echoes the swirl of the gray metal curtain pole.

1 Stick strips of low-tack masking tape in a line around the edge of the canvas rug, about 2in (5cm) from the edge. Stick another line of tape around the rug, about 10in (25cm) in from the first line. This is to enable you to paint a straight-edged border around the rug.

2 Mix up some pink glaze with I part pink latex paint and 2 parts water-based varnish. Lightly dab a sponge first into the glaze, then on to the masked-off border. Continue sponging pink glaze around the rug until the entire border is a soft mottled pink.

3 Draw a simple stencil design on thick paper. This one reflects the design of the metal curtain pole. Place the paper on a cutting mat and, using a craft knife, carefully cut out the design.

4 Position the stencil over the border of the canvas rug. Using gray spray paint, lightly spray through the stencil on to the border.

5 Keeping the stencil in position, stipple aqua paint through the stencil on top of the gray color to give a more metallic feel. Allow some of the gray color to show through.

6 Go over the stenciled motif with patches of gold paint, rubbing it on with a finger for an aged look. Continue to stencil in this way around the border of the rug. Then remove the masking tape to reveal the completed stenciled decoration. Allow the paint to dry thoroughly before using the rug.

Revamping an iron bed frame

cast-iron bed frame

bowl

rubber gloves

cloth or scrubbing brush

coarse-grit sandpaper

all-purpose paintbrush

all-purpose water-based primer or antirust primer

latex paint: white, pink, pistachio

fine artist's brush

soft cloth

medium-grit sandpaper

raw umber paint pigment

water-based varnish

dragging brush

silver metallic paint

You might think that it is all very well being tempted to buy an old jug from a junk shop, because you know that prior to it taking up pride of place on your dresser it will be thoroughly washed or dusted down. However, if the piece you intend to purchase is likely to be the weight of a small cart horse and rusty as well, the idea of cleaning such a large object might not be so appealing. However, this project shows that with a little determination and some elbow grease, it is quite possible to rescue and revamp a large cast-iron bed frame, thus combining the elegance of an age gone by with the comfort and convenience of today's lifestyle.

1 Before tackling the rot or damage to a cast-iron bed frame you need to remove all the surface dust and dirt. Fill a large bowl with warm soapy water and use a cloth to wash away as much of the loose paintwork as you can; alternatively, a stiff scrubbing brush will help with this.

2 Allow the bed frame to dry, then rub it vigorously with coarse-grit sandpaper to remove any remaining rust and old paintwork.

3 Using an all-purpose paintbrush, apply a coat of all-purpose water-based primer over the entire bed frame. Alternatively, if there is rust present on the frame, use antirust primer instead. Allow to dry.

4 Paint a coat of white latex paint over the whole bed frame, watching out for any runs or drips. Let dry, then apply a second coat if necessary for an even all-over coverage.

5 Using a fine artist's brush, paint any details or features of the bed in pink latex paint.

6 Using a soft cloth, rub away some of the paint on the details to create the look of wear and tear.

7 Paint fine lines of pistachio-colored latex paint over the details to highlight the intricate metalwork. Allow the paint to dry thoroughly.

8 Using medium-grit sandpaper, rub down the paintwork on the bed frame to reveal patches of previous paint layers, and in some areas bare metal. This will add to the aged and worn feel that an old bed would almost certainly have.

9 Make some aging glaze by mixing a tablespoon of raw umber paint pigment in a pot of water-based varnish. Brush a coat of aging glaze over the frame using a long-haired soft dragging brush. Allow the glaze to pool in some areas, but do not allow any runs to occur.

10 Using a fine artist's brush, apply silver metallic paint to any intricate moldings to highlight and accentuate these areas. Allow to dry.

EXPERT TIPS

• *It is a good idea to wear rubber gloves for protection when scrubbing down the bed frame.*

• *Although it is fun to use color on an old bed, it is probably best to confine its use to very small areas and to tone it down with the use of aging glaze if the bed is to have any real authenticity. Bright colors can look too garish on an old bed.*

• *Dress a cast-iron bed with either antique or reproduction lace sheets and some large, square, lace-edged pillows, or use an antique patchwork quilt as a bedspread, combined with an array of differently patterned pillows.*

MATERIALS

padded bedspread

sewing thread

sewing machine

tape measure

silk flowers

tape measure

ribbons for tieback

dressmaker's shears

pins

2 brass rings

pencil

awl

hanging hook

nail

hammer

Bedspread curtain and tieback

In this project, a simple curtain is created from a bedspread, while ribbons and silk flowers, normally seen adorning hats on holidays, are used in an unusual decoration for a curtain tieback. In this pale room, which is continually flooded with light, the window dressing needed to be simple but also to exclude light. The solution came in the shape of a soft quilted antique bedspread that was double-sided with padding in between, therefore negating the need to line or interline. The bedspread was cream on one side and a soft pink appliqué on the other, so when the top was folded over to create a loop to feed on to the curtain pole, there was an instant design. A simple ribbon tieback to hold back the quilt curtain for daytime use allows a glimpse of the decorative silk flowers.

EXPERT TIPS
- *When looking for a quilt or bedspread that might double up as a curtain, do not use anything that is too thick or unevenly padded as the light passing through it will show this up.*

- *If you find a beautiful antique, make sure that it is both strong enough to be tugged open and closed and has no evidence of wear and tear that would be noticeable when hung up. Remember also that you might need a pair of curtains.*

1 Fold over the top of the bedspread to make a loop of fabric that the curtain pole can be slipped through. Baste the fabric layers, then machine stitch to secure. At measured intervals, hand-stitch the silk flowers and ribbons to the bedspread top.

2 Calculate the length of tieback you will need. Measure the distance from where you will position the hook on the wall around the curtain and back to the hook again. Then cut the length of ribbon accordingly. If your ribbon is thin, back it with a more robust one. Lay the ribbon flat, and pin the narrower ribbon on the top and machine-sew around the edge. Tie a large bow in the center of the ribbon. Stitch the silk flowers into position on one side of the ribbon.

3 Attach a brass ring to each side of the tieback. Fold each ribbon end by ½in (12mm). Lay the ring on the folded end, fold back the ribbon to enclose the ring. Then stitch the ribbon to secure.

4 Position the tieback around the curtain and mark with a pencil cross on the wall the position of the tieback hook. Using an awl, make a small dent in the wall in the center of the cross.

5 Attach the hanging hook to the wall by carefully tapping a nail through the hole in the hook. Then simply slip the tieback rings over the hook to hold back the curtain.

MAKEOVER   PROJECT

Lemon'n Lime

This sunny color scheme of lemon and lime is fresh, clean, youthful, and invigorating. In this bedroom, you will want to leap out of bed in the morning, full of vitality and enthusiasm for the day ahead.

Although paint has miraculous transforming abilities, sometimes the desire to use a much-loved wallpaper is just too tempting, and this combination of lemon and lime checks has always been a favorite. Many home decorators are reluctant to attempt to hang their own wallpaper.

PROJECTS FROM THIS
MAKEOVER SHOW YOU

- HOW TO PREPARE AND
  HANG WALLPAPER

- HOW TO DECORATE
  WITH WALLPAPER

- HOW TO MAKE FROSTED
  GLASSES

- HOW TO MAKE A
  PILLOW WITH TIES

- HOW TO PAINT A
  PICTURE FRAME

But if care is taken and a methodical approach is followed, there is no reason why anyone should be discouraged.

In this room two different colors of the same wallpaper were used. The checked paper is available in lemon and lime: the lemon was used on the ceiling and the lime on the walls. The cornice was dragged in a deep lime green and the woodwork was painted in turquoise. The window and door moldings were painted light lime green. The bed was dragged in pale lemon and the table and clothes dryer were painted turquoise. The accessories picked up on the checks and lemon and lime scheme.

PREPARATION

Before wallpapering your room, remove the old wallpaper and repair any damage done to the wall surface in so doing. Treat any damp patches, as failure to deal with them at this stage will be expensive if the staining appears later through the new wallpaper.

Paste lining paper on the walls prior to hanging wallpaper. This should be pasted on horizontally rather than vertically; this evens out any odd lumps and bulges in the wall, and keeps them from showing through the wallpaper, making for an uneven finish.

HANGING WALLPAPER

Take your time when hanging wallpaper for the first time. Although it may look easy, achieving a neat finish with patterns matching and no trapped air bubbles takes a bit of planning and care. Unroll the wallpaper and measure out your required length; do not underestimate the drop. If you intend to use striped wallpaper, it is crucial that the first piece be hung vertically straight.

EXPERT TIPS

• *When papering around an arch, trim, cut, and then fold the paper over to fit around the curve. Use a final strip of wallpaper to disguise the flaps.*

• *Scaffold boards suspended between stepladders will give you a safe and sturdy base from which to reach ceilings and inaccessible corners.*

1 Make sure the wallpaper pattern is both vertically and horizontally correct. Brush wallpaper paste over the back of the wallpaper. Place the wallpaper on the prepared wall surface. Then, using a dry, clean brush and applying gentle downward pressure, stroke the wallpaper smoothly into position. Brush out any air bubbles that are trapped between the wall and the paper.

2 Where the wallpaper meets and overhangs the baseboard, gently push the wallpaper into the corner to make a neat, straight fold. Using the wallpaper shears, score along the folded edge to enable you to trim away the excess wallpaper.

3 Gently peel back the wallpaper at the base and, using the shears, cut cleanly along the scored line. Take care not to leave any ragged edges or rip the paper. Either discard the excess wallpaper or put it to one side for making wallpaper scallops (see page 42).

4 Using the dry papering brush, push the wallpaper back against the wall. Gently scrub the paper into the corner with the edge of the brush. Using a soft damp cloth, wipe away any residue of paste that may be left on either the wallpaper or the baseboard.

MATERIALS

dinner plate

wallpaper

masking tape

pencil

cutting mat or
cardboard

craft knife

saucer

pinking shears

wallpaper paste

Making scallops and wallpaper decoration

This project uses leftover pieces of wallpaper to create a border of scallops along the base of the cornice, and flower motifs around the window, to add to the decorative feel of the room. As well as involving little or no outlay, these ideas can be used to liven up a piece of furniture, or to make your own border or chair rail.

1 To create a scalloped border from wallpaper, place a dinner plate over the edge of a piece of wallpaper so that it is half on the paper. Mark the halfway point on each side of the plate with a strip of masking tape. Draw around the curved plate with a pencil. Continue to draw scalloped curves along the paper, always lining up the edge of the paper with the masking tape on the plate.

2 Place a cutting mat or piece of cardboard under the wallpaper to protect your work surface. Using a craft knife, carefully cut along the penciled curves to create a row of scallops, taking care not to cut through to the edge of the wallpaper. The scalloped border can now be pasted directly under the cornice.

3 Find two circular objects you can draw around; one should be larger than the other. Here we have used a saucer and a reel of masking tape. Draw around the saucer on lemon-checked wallpaper. This circle will form the basis of the flower head.

4 Draw a simple flower shape. The petals should extend no farther than the original circle. Add a stalk and a pair of leaves. Then place the masking tape in the center and draw around it. Place the tape on green-checked wallpaper. Draw around the inside of it.

5 Using pinking shears to create an appliquéd effect, cut out the center section of the flower motif, and the rest of the flower motif from the lemon-checked wallpaper.

6 Using wallpaper paste, stick the flower design on to the wall, pressing it from the center outward to remove air bubbles. Cut smaller leaves from the green-checked paper and stick these on top of the yellow leaves. Repeat the process for further flower motifs.

43

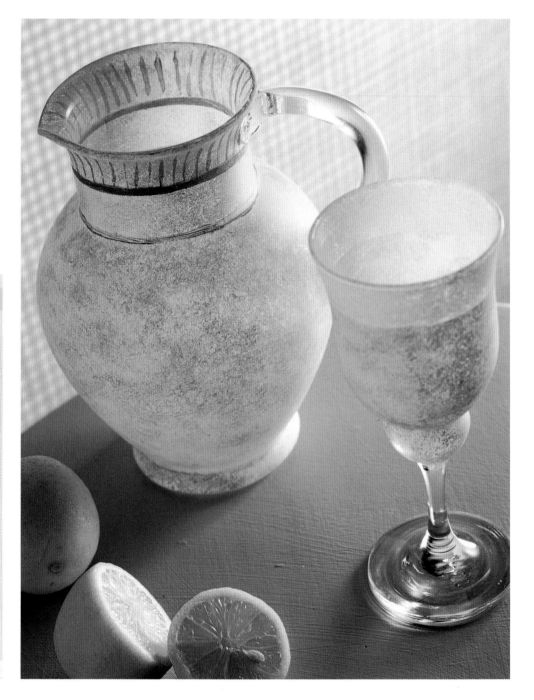

MATERIALS

glassware

soft cloth

denatured alcohol

masking tape

sponge

white latex paint

water-based varnish

acrylic paint: yellow, blue

stippling brush

fine pointed soft brush

water-based spray
varnish

Frosting glassware

Decorating glassware with this frosting technique is a quick and easy way to transform ordinary glass jugs or bowls into ornamental pieces for your home. Using little more than a can of latex flat paint and some water-based varnish, you will be able to frost your glassware to match your decor. Once you have tried the following few simple steps, you can go on to design your own exciting patterns.

EXPERT TIP

• *Although these finished pieces of glassware look like frosted glass, you must remember that this is a decorative technique only. Rough handling of the glass or washing it in hot water will cause the paint to peel off eventually. If a more permanent and practical use is needed, you can purchase special glass paints, which offer a water-resistant quality.*

1 Wash the glass object thoroughly in hot soapy water, then rinse under the hot tap. Allow to dry completely and then wipe the whole surface with a clean soft cloth and denatured alcohol to remove any remaining grease. Using masking tape, mask off any area that you wish to remain as clear glass.

2 Dip a small piece of sponge into white latex paint, then dab the sponge lightly all over the surface of the unmasked glass to achieve an even covering. Allow to dry completely.

3 Mix up a glaze using a small quantity of water-based varnish and a blob of yellow acrylic paint. Then, using a stippling brush, jab the glaze over the top of the dry latex paint on the glass. Let dry completely.

4 Gently peel away the masking tape. Then sponge a white base coat over the clear glass and, when dry, stipple over a complementary-color glaze as shown in step 3. Alternatively, you can leave the glass clear.

5 Allow the paint to dry completely. Using a fine pointed soft brush, add further details over the top of the stippled paint in blue acrylic paint, covering the join of the two contrasting colors. Allow to dry, then spray the glass with clear varnish for protection.

Making a pillow with ties

pillow form

tape measure

fabric for pillow cover

tailor's chalk

dressmaker's shears or pinking shears

fabric for piping and ties

piping cord

basting thread

pins

sewing machine

matching thread

iron

You can never have too many pillows, especially in a bedroom. These items of soft furnishing add a touch of softness and comfort to even the most austere of rooms, which in turn creates a relaxing environment. At the very least they can be used as excellent injury-free weapons in a child's room! This easy project features a practical square pillow made with decorative fabric ties. The use of two complementry fabrics—lime check and cobalt blue check—adds both a sassy design quality and a sense of fun. If you prefer, you could use up odds and ends of fabric that you may have around.

1 Measure the pillow form. Allowing ¾in (2cm) extra all around, measure and mark up two squares of fabric using tailor's chalk, and a smaller piece 2⅜in (6cm) long and the same width as the squares for the flap. Cut out the pieces with dressmaker's shears. Then cut out contrasting fabric for the piping; this should be 1½in (4cm) wide and as long as the outer edge of the cover.

2 To make the piping, fold the contrasting strip in half lengthwise and place piping cord into the fold. Run a basting stitch through the fabric and cord to hold it in place. Then pin this around the edge of one of the fabric squares, raw edges matching, and machine-stitch in position.

3 To make the pillow ties, first cut out four pieces of contrasting fabric 8in (20cm) long and 4in (10cm) wide. Fold each piece lengthwise with right sides facing, then turn under the raw edges, and baste and machine-stitch around the three sides. Turn the ties the right way out and press with a warm iron to neaten.

4 Turn under and stitch one edge of the unpiped fabric square. Place two ties on this edge. Baste, then machine-stitch in place.

5 Match up the remaining ties on the edge of the piped fabric square; pin in place. Place the small flap of fabric over these ties against the edge of the square, right sides facing, enclosing the ties. Pin, baste, and machine-stitch the layers together to create an envelope-type flap.

6 Place the other fabric square on top of these layers, right sides together and the ties matching. Pin, baste, and stitch around the remaining three sides of the pillow cover. Turn the cover the right side out through the flap. Insert the pillow form and arrange the ties to finish.

MATERIALS

wooden frame

water-based all-purpose
primer

all-purpose paintbrush

fine-grit sandpaper

latex paint: blue,
lime green

masking tape

small paintbrush

turquoise paint

water-based satin finish
varnish

Painting a picture frame

If you have ever wasted precious time in a picture frame store trying to select the right frame for a much-loved piece of art, then this is the project for you. It was only after years of disappointing results in choosing suitable frames that it became clear that the best results could be achieved by adapting and painting the frame yourself. In this way the frame can be colored to enhance the image it frames and to coordinate with your chosen interior. In this project a plain wooden frame was adapted with the use of paint and masking tape to make a frame that relates well not only to the painting but also to its environment. Plain untreated wooden frames are often cheaper than gilt, lacquered, or gesso ones, and they also offer you the opportunity to change the frame color as often as you choose.

1 Brush a coat of water-based all-purpose primer over the entire frame. This will seal the wood and cover any knots that may occur naturally in the wood of the frame. Allow to dry.

2 Rub the primed frame with fine-grit sandpaper to smooth the surface, then paint the frame with blue latex paint. To achieve a hand-painted look, drag the paint on over the white primer, allowing some of the white primer to show through.

3 Allow the paint to dry. Then mask off the inner and outer edges of the frame with masking tape, leaving only the middle section visible.

4 Carefully apply lime green paint to the section of frame between the two masked edges. As before, drag the paint over the area, allowing the blue base coat to show through in fine lines. Allow the paint to dry.

5 Remove the masking tape carefully so as not to take the paint layer with it. If any paint is pulled off, touch up the area with a small dab of blue paint. Then rub the whole frame with fine-grit sandpaper. Using a small paintbrush, paint thin lines of turquoise paint on the raised edges of the frame. Allow to dry, then seal the frame with a coat of water-based satin finish varnish.

EXPERT TIPS

• *If you intend to paint a frame that you already have, remove the painting prior to priming. If this is not possible, protect the painting by covering it with paper and masking around the frame's inside edge.*

• *Try your hand at more adventurous paint effects on your frames, such as rag rolling or sponging. Often a combination of paint effects can work very well.*

Moody Blues

The range of different blues used in this color scheme creates a slightly turbulent light, giving the room a moody, atmospheric quality. The addition of white in the color scheme softens and freshens the overall feel.

Blue is a very popular color for bedrooms; we may all like our beds to be warm but on the whole we like the actual room to be cool. With the invention of central heating, the use of blue in decorating schemes has increased. The inspiration for this room emerged from waking in the night to

PROJECTS FROM THIS
MAKEOVER SHOW YOU

- HOW TO PAINT
  ADJOINING SURFACES

- HOW TO PAINT A
  FLOOR

- HOW TO MAKE A
  PADDED PICTURE
  FRAME

- HOW TO DECORATE
  CERAMICS

catch the last of the rolling thunder, when flashes of electric blue light streaked into the room. There is the most amazing sense of calm after a storm. This makeover is an attempt to regain that feeling of exhilaration.

As blue is a receding color, seeming to create space, you can apply the paint flat without the fear of reflective intensity. In this room the walls and ceiling were painted a warm medium blue, the window and door a deep cobalt blue, and the woodwork a medium lavender blue. The cornice was painted slightly unevenly in a pale lilac blue, while the floor was given a distressed finish in cool sea blue.

PREPARATION

Stick down any loose wallpaper with wallpaper paste, and fill any cracks in the plaster with filler. As the room will be painted with flat latex paint, pay particular attention to the condition of the walls. Make sure that they are thoroughly rubbed down and smoothed prior to painting, otherwise imperfections will show up clearly. When painting with different blues, make sure that the colors do not overlap; careful masking is essential.

Choose your accessories for the bedroom carefully. In this room, white was used together with punchy checked fabrics, which are widely available in stores. They add a warming sense of welcome to what could otherwise be an austere environment.

PAINTING ADJOINING SURFACES

When painting a cornice in a different color from the ceiling and walls, it is essential to mask off the surfaces on either side of it. This will ensure that paint does not spatter on the ceiling or wall, and that the painted edges of the cornice are straight and even. Choose a color of paint that works well with the adjoining surfaces to avoid clashing. Here, the cornice is painted in pale lilac blue while the adjoining walls are painted in medium blue.

EXPERT TIPS

• *If patches or stains appear on a newly painted surface, this might indicate poor preparation. Mineral salts in fresh plaster can leach through inadequately sealed and primed surfaces. Likewise, damp and mold can also seep through. If this occurs, repaint the surface using an appropriate primer sealer; only when this has dried thoroughly can the top coat be reapplied.*

• *When covering a dark-toned surface with a lighter color, apply the paint evenly and generously to keep the paint from leaving a streaky finish. If this does occur, apply further coats until an even top coat is achieved.*

1 Stick lengths of low-tack masking tape along the edges of the ceiling and wall adjoining the cornice.

2 Using an all-purpose brush, paint the cornice with pale lilac blue latex paint, taking care that the brushstrokes are confined within the lengths of masking tape to produce a clean straight edge. Allow the paint to dry thoroughly.

3 Remove the masking tape and reapply it on the painted cornice, butting it up to the edge of the wall. Then apply medium blue latex paint on the wall right up to the cornice to produce a clean straight edge with no overlapping of color.

Painting a floor

MATERIALS

hammer

coarse-grit sandpaper

water-based all-purpose primer

all-purpose brushes

latex paint: pink, sea blue, creamy yellow

large soft brush

floor varnish

Floor painting can be the ideal answer to matching up a variety of paint colors in a room. It also lends itself to a wide and varied choice of application. There is a huge range of commercial colors available; alternatively, colors can be hand-mixed with limitless possibilities. Colors can be laid on top of one another to build up different decorative effects. Any number of designs can be used to enhance or contrast with your already existing color theme. A new floor can be antiqued or an old one brought up to date. With the use of contemporary floor varnishes widely available, there is no reason why your painted floor should not last forever.

1 Inspect the floorboards before you begin and hammer down any prominent nail heads. Then rub the floor vigorously with coarse-grit sandpaper wrapped around a block of wood to create a smooth surface. Pay particular attention to boards that are warped or split. Paint the floor with water-based all-purpose primer and allow to dry.

2 Using an all-purpose brush, apply a base coat of pink latex paint over the floorboards, dragging the brush over the surface to produce long brushstrokes. Allow to dry.

3 Dip a large soft brush into sea blue latex paint, then drag it over the base coat, allowing some of the pink to show through. Let dry.

4 Using a smaller all-purpose brush, apply creamy yellow latex paint intermittently along the floorboards, carefully following the line of the grain and the previous brushmarks.

5 When the paint is thoroughly dry, apply two coats of long-wearing floor varnish to seal and protect the aged and distressed floor. Allow the first coat to dry before applying the second. Allow the varnish to dry completely before walking on the floor.

MATERIALS

image

ruler

pencil

thin cardboard

scissors

strong cardboard

fabric

tailor's chalk

dressmaker's shears,
optional

craft knife

interfacing

fabric glue

double-sided tape

Perspex

transparent tape

Making a padded frame

Almost everyone has a favorite picture or photograph, yet it can be difficult finding the right frame to display it. As a result, the picture may be left propped between objects on a shelf, collecting dust and gradually becoming more dog-eared and scratched. This project solves the problem by showing you how to make your own picture or photo frame, which can be covered in a fabric of your choice to match your decorative color scheme. This will add a homey touch to any image and, whether it stands alone or as part of a collection, it will definitely enhance your bedroom.

1 Measure the image. Draw a square on thin cardboard slightly larger than the image. Then draw a square around this one 1¼in (3cm) larger all around. Draw two more squares the same size as the outer square. Cut out the three large squares. Cut a wedge-shaped frame support from strong cardboard.

2 Place one cardboard square on your chosen fabric. Allowing for a ¾in (2cm) turnover, mark the fabric all around the square with tailor's chalk. Repeat to mark a second square. Cut out the fabric squares using dressmaker's shears. Then cut out enough fabric to cover the cardboard frame support.

3 Cut out the square window from the first cardboard square. Cut two pieces of interfacing and glue these to the cardboard frame. Glue one fabric square over the padding, wrapping the edges over the back. Cut a diagonal cross in the fabric over the window. Glue the fabric triangles to the back of the cardboard.

4 Lay the remaining fabric square face down and place a second cardboard square on top. Fold and stick the edges of the fabric on the cardboard securely. Apply glue over the side of the cardboard with the fabric overlap and place the remaining cardboard square on top. Attach the image to the center of this square with double-sided tape.

5 Stick a piece of Perspex to the inside of the window using transparent tape. Apply glue to the cardboard surrounding the image and press the fabric-covered window frame on top, padded side uppermost. Stick fabric to the frame support with fabric glue, then glue the support to the back of the frame with the aid of a small cardboard hinge.

EXPERT TIPS

• *Choose fabric appropriate to the scale of the frame, as a large-patterned fabric will be lost on a small-sized frame.*

• *Use fast-drying fabric glue and wash your hands between each step to avoid ruining the fabric of the frame.*

Painting ceramics

MATERIALS

ceramics

masking tape

fine artist's brush

ceramic paint

low-tack masking tape

solvent

cotton swab

paper dots

stippling brush

When you change the color scheme of your bedroom and go to the trouble of finding new fabrics and lighting, it is often not possible to reuse existing accessories because they just do not match the new scheme. This project gives you a chance to redesign or change in as dramatic a way as you like any of those favorite jugs, bowls, cups, and saucers that do not fit in with your decor. Painting ceramics is both inexpensive and satisfying to do, as it recycles old ceramics as well as provides an excuse to vent your artistic skills, however limited they might be. In these examples artistic flair is unnecessary, as using masking tape makes it easy to add decorative stripes and checks to transform plain ceramics instantly.

EXPERT TIP

• *Paint effects such as sponging or dragging can work well on ceramics when they are combined with masking or stenciling.*

1 Wash the ceramic piece and make sure that your hands are clean and free of grease; any grease on the ceramic piece will result in the paint being repelled. Dry the ceramic piece thoroughly. For a checked design, stick lengths of masking tape in vertical stripes around the side of your ceramic piece, leaving a gap of approximately ½in (12mm) between each length.

2 Using a pointed fine artist's brush, apply medium blue ceramic paint over the unmasked areas. Allow to dry, then peel off the masking tape. Remask the ceramic piece with horizontal bands (this time low-tack tape), again leaving ½in (12mm) between each band. Paint darker blue ceramic paint over the unmasked areas. Clean off any spillovers of paint with solvent and a cotton swab.

3 Allow the paint to dry, then peel off the masking tape carefully. If any paint pulls off, apply a few dabs of paint over the top to repair the damage.

4 To create a spotted design, place paper dots randomly over the piece. Stipple ceramic paint on the surface to cover it completely. Let dry, then carefully peel off the paper dots to reveal clean white ceramic spots underneath. Clean off any unwanted glaze with a cotton swab. If desired, you can paint in the white dots with a contrasting color.

MAKEOVER PROJECT

Rich Terra-cotta

Terra-cotta evokes sunlight and heat, and the rich terra-cotta walls in this color scheme create a warm, cosy atmosphere, ideal for a bedroom. The blue floorboards complement the walls and soften the effect of the terra-cotta.

Terra-cotta is a very popular color, perhaps because it evokes those exotic warm countries where terra-cotta is so often used and where you can see and appreciate the wonderful effect and depth that the use of this rich warm color can offer. Collect a few old terra-cotta pots together

 Dry-brushing and aging woodwork • Making a découpaged tr

PROJECTS FROM THIS
MAKEOVER SHOW YOU

- HOW TO DRY-BRUSH
  AND AGE SURFACES

- HOW TO MAKE A
  DÉCOUPAGED *TROMPE-
  L'OEIL* JUG

- HOW TO ANTIQUE
  WOODEN SHUTTERS

and examine their colors; you will see that terra-cotta is actually composed of a range of brownish orange colors. Use a few colors and blend them together.

As the walls were the dominant part of this room, they were decorated with a terra-cotta color wash. A color wash imitates the appearance of old-fashioned, distemper-painted walls, and this paint effect gives the room a sunny, bleached atmosphere, exactly what was wanted in this texture-rich natural interior. Color-washing is an easy technique to do and a very useful technique if the wall surface is at all lumpy or irregular.

PREPARATION

When color-washing, lots of liquid may be splashed around the room, so make sure that any furnishings that cannot be removed are covered with both dust sheets and polyethylene to protect them from staining. Also see that any electrical outlets, such as sockets, are switched off, the plugs removed, and the outlets covered in polyethylene and sealed with masking tape.

If the walls are in good decorative order and are painted white or another suitable tone, then all that is required is to wash the walls well with a sponge and a bowl of warm water. This should remove any dirt and dust. If there are any greasy patches, remove them with a general household cleaner prior to color-washing.

If the walls are a dark color, they will require priming prior to being color-washed. If drips and runs occur when priming, and these cannot be blended in using a clean damp brush, allow the area to dry completely and then reprime, taking care to blend the primer at the edges. This should help disguise the area and diffuse any darker patches.

DRY-BRUSHING AND AGING

These techniques are easy to do following the steps below. They are also useful when decorating woodwork as they add depth and texture to what would otherwise be areas of flat color.

EXPERT TIPS

• *Try to maintain as high a standard of cleanliness as possible when using paint effects. Always make sure that you have a clean rag by your side; use this to wipe away any runs in the paint or remove any overlaps before they dry.*

• *Always clean out any mixing vessels thoroughly, as residues can react with other colors causing a discoloring effect.*

1 Mask off the wall and floor on either side of the surface to be painted. Mix a wash using 1 part pale gray latex paint and 3 parts water-based varnish, then add a little water until the mixture is like milk. Apply a base coat of the pale gray wash.

2 Allow the base coat to dry. Then dip a dry brush into deeper gray paint and drag this over the base coat, allowing streaks of the pale gray to show through. Let dry.

3 Mix aging glaze by adding a small amount of burnt umber pigment to water-based varnish. Add more pigment as required to achieve the desired depth of tone. Brush the aging glaze over the painted surface and let dry.

LONDON PUBLIC LIBRARY
20 EAST FIRST STREET
LONDON, OHIO 43140

Découpaged jug

MATERIALS

paper

water-based all-purpose primer

all-purpose brush

pencil

cutting mat or cardboard

craft knife

latex paint: terra-cotta, brown, green

water-based varnish

artist's brushes

varnish brush

Découpage is the cutting out and sticking down of paper decoration, and it is a good alternative to stenciling. This project shows how to make a paper terra-cotta jug to use as a *trompe-l'oeil* decoration on a bedroom wall. You can either stick or simply lean your flat jug against the wall to create a piece of decorative fun.

EXPERT TIPS

• *If you don't want to paint a decoration for your wall, cut out an image from a book or magazine. Glue this to a piece of cardboard, trim around the edges, then varnish over the top and use as shown.*

• *Create your own family portrait by photocopying photos. Brush with aging glaze to create a sepia tone, then affix to the wall. Hang a silver-sprayed cardboard frame over the image.*

1 Paint a piece of paper with water-based all-purpose primer; paper will discolor if left unprotected, so a coat of primer will not only help to prevent damage but also make a good surface to work on. Using a pencil, draw or trace the outline of your image on the paper.

2 Place the paper on a cutting mat or piece of cardboard to protect the underlying work surface. Then, using a craft knife, carefully cut out the penciled shape, working slowly and turning the paper as you go to retain the soft curves of the design.

3 Mix up a diluted wash of 1 part terra-cotta latex paint to 3 parts water-based varnish. When mixed thoroughly, add a little water until the mixture is the consistency of milk. Using an artist's brush, paint the cut-out jug with the terra-cotta wash to establish a three-dimensional effect.

4 Using a finer artist's brush, add patches of brown and green latex paint to shade the sides of the jug, highlight the rim, and emphasize the jug's curved shape. Keep stepping back from to judge the effect, correcting any details as necessary as you are painting.

5 Allow the paint to dry, then apply a coat of water-based varnish over the top to protect the image. Allow the découpaged jug to dry flat.

Antiquing wooden shutters

MATERIALS

wooden shutters

fine-grit and coarse-grit
sandpaper

cloth

all-purpose paintbrush

terra-cotta latex satin
paint

fine artist's brush

dark brown latex
paint

burnt umber acrylic
paint

satin finish water-based
varnish

Aged and antiqued wooden shutters immediately create a look that is reminiscent of vacations in foreign lands and exciting times. When used in a room like this, they add a distinct air of authenticity. Sometimes shutters are preferable for a window for practical reasons, for instance in a bathroom with a large sash window to the front, where partial privacy is required. Shutters can offer the same privacy, warmth, and light control as other, more traditional, forms of window dressing, but at the same time they create a more unusual or architectural finish. Antiquing shutters is a simple and effective way of linking a decorating theme such as the Mediterranean, sun-soaked feel of this room. The following step-by-step guide shows you how to go about antiquing a pair of shutters.

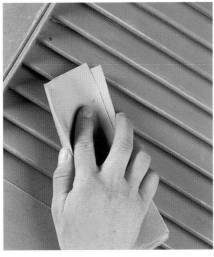

EXPERT TIPS

• *To avoid drips when painting shutters, work with as dry a brush as possible; do not overload the brush with paint. Turn the shutter as you are applying paint as this gives you an opportunity to catch and disperse any runs as they occur.*

• *When applying the final aging glaze, it is better to apply two or three lighter coats of glaze rather than one heavy brown coat, which can be the result of overzealous quantities of burnt umber being added to the initial glaze.*

1 Rub the shutters lightly with fine-grit sandpaper, then wipe them with a damp cloth to remove any dust. Using an all-purpose paintbrush, apply a coat of terra-cotta latex satin paint over each shutter, taking care to catch any drips or runs. Check that as the paint is applied to one side of the louvers no paint is pooling on the other side.

2 When the paint is completely dry—usually two hours or so—rub the shutters vigorously with coarse-grit sandpaper, turning the shutters as you work to give an even feel. Then rub the edges of the shutter frame with sandpaper to remove sections of paint completely; this will create an impression of natural wear and tear.

3 With a fine artist's brush, apply patches of dark brown latex paint to the heavily sanded areas and rub this in with your finger. This will create the effect of old wood under the terra-cotta paintwork. Then continue to sand and scrape at the paint until a satisfactory look is achieved.

4 Mix some aging glaze by adding a blob of burnt umber acrylic paint to a can of satin finish water-based varnish, mixing thoroughly. Apply this in sweeping brushstrokes across the louvers and around the frame in a counterclockwise direction. Allow to dry, then apply a coat of clear varnish for protection.

Neutral Tones

The muted tones of cream, vanilla, and pale, sultry gray featured in this decorating scheme, balanced with the simplicity and understatement of the furnishings, have created an effect of elegance and sophistication. This is a bedroom to lounge around in wearing sheer silk pajamas, should you have the inclination.

The inspiration for this room evolved from many sources: old French novels and films, antique cotton lace sheets, a small ceramic cherub rescued from a flea market, and a soft white rose

PROJECTS FROM THIS
MAKEOVER SHOW YOU

- HOW TO SPONGE A
  WALL

- HOW TO ANTIQUE A
  TABLE

- HOW TO MAKE A FABRIC
  LAMPSHADE

- HOW TO SEW LAVENDER
  SACHETS

still glistening with dew. When these objects were collected together, paint color chips were consulted and the choice of soft shades of vanilla, lily white, cream, and pale gray emerged. It also became obvious that part of the attraction of these inspirational objects was their timeworn appearance, and so it was important that this be also reflected in the room, to create the impression of faded elegance.

The paint was applied with differing techniques, thus avoiding any hard edges or defining lines. Subtle tones of color were used, and no aspect of the room was overstated. The effect is a soft blending of colors.

PREPARATION

Before you begin to paint, go over the ceiling, walls, and woodwork to check for peeling paper, air bubbles, and any cracks. Stick any loose paper back in position with wallpaper paste. Cut any air bubbles and stick back in position with paste. This is especially important for ceilings; if loose paper is painted over, the weight of the wet paint might cause it to tear and fall, bringing with it a section of ceiling plaster. Fill in any cracks with all-purpose filler, allow to dry, then sand to a smooth finish. This preparation is essential to ensure a smooth finish.

Prepare your paint colors in readiness for using them. The use of neutral colors has always been popular; pale tones can be a sound starting point for adding extra color, which can be gently added at any stage.

SPONGING A WALL

Before sponging a wall, you must first prime it with water-based all-purpose primer. This seals the surface and provides a good surface on which to apply glaze. If the surface is not sealed, the glaze will soak into the wall and ruin the effect. In this makeover, the walls and ceiling weredelicately sponged in a pale vanilla paint and water-based glaze over a white primed surface.

EXPERT TIP

• *When using water-based varnish, allow yourself enough time and material to cover whole sections. If the telephone rings when you are halfway across the wall, let it ring. If you stop a paint effect in full flow, you will return to a distinctive line. This will become worse when you begin again and retrace your steps, making the line even deeper in tone.*

1 Using an all-purpose brush, paint the wall surface with water-based all-purpose primer. Apply the primer in all directions, up and down, side to side and diagonally so that brushmarks are not visible. Make sure the coverage is even. Allow to dry.

2 In a pot, mix together 1 part pale vanilla latex paint with 2 parts water-based varnish. Use a paintbrush to stir the mixture together well; this is the sponging glaze.

3 Dip a sponge lightly into the vanilla glaze, then dab the sponge on the wall to create a pattern of small dots. Continue to dab the sponge over the surface, dipping it into the glaze as needed, until the entire wall is covered in a soft, mottled paint effect.

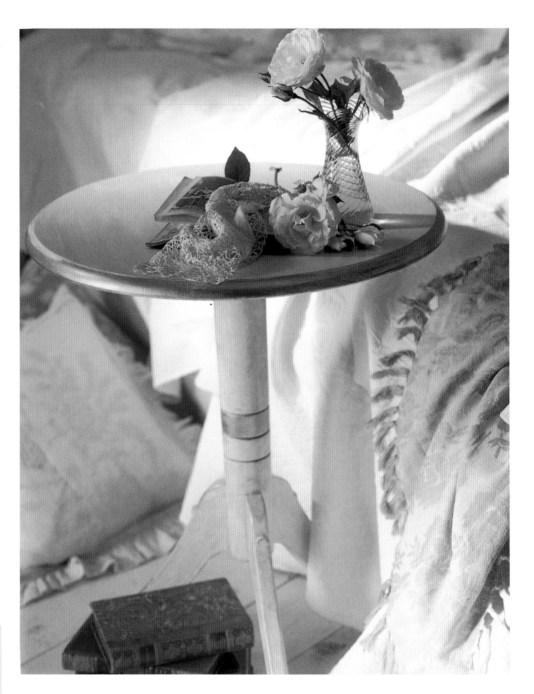

MATERIALS

wooden table

sandpaper

water-based all-purpose
primer

all-purpose brush

white latex paint

burnt umber pigment

water-based varnish

gold paint

Antiquing a table

Antiquing produces and imitates the effects of time on paint and adds a worn look to the newest of pieces, creating a mellow blend between genuinely old and new. This small pine occasional table was transformed into a delightful piece that, when intermingled with other genuine antiques in the room, adds a degree of elegance and charm. It also has the added advantage of being user friendly and, because of the water-based varnish, knock resistant.

1 Rub the table with sandpaper wrapped around a block to smooth the surface and give it a key to enable the paint to adhere. Then prime it with water-based all-purpose primer to seal the surface, making sure that the table is evenly covered. Allow to dry.

2 When the primer is thoroughly dry, rub the table lightly with sandpaper so that small patches of the original surface show through the primer.

3 Using an all-purpose brush, apply a coat of white latex paint thinly and evenly over the entire table. Let dry, then sand the surface very lightly again for a smooth finish.

4 Mix the aging glaze by adding a small amount of burnt umber pigment to water-based varnish. Add more pigment as required to achieve the desired depth of tone. Brush the glaze over the surface of the table and allow to dry completely.

5 Dip a finger in gold paint and rub it roughly around the edge of the tabletop to imitate gilt edging. Add a further gold band around the table leg if desired. The intermittent application of the gold emulates the natural wear on the edge of the table. The end result might not fool an antiques expert but it will look authentic in a room scheme such as this.

EXPERT TIPS

• *For an authentic look, make sure that the table is completely sealed with several coats of water-based varnish, sanding with fine-grit sandpaper between each coat.*

• *If the table is to receive heavy use, cut a glass or Perspex top to protect the table surface.*

73

Making a fabric lampshade

MATERIALS

lampshade frame

tape measure

fabric

dressmaker's shears

iron

pins

sewing thread

sewing machine

tailor's chalk

pom-pom fringing

craft knife

tapestry needle or safety pin

ribbon or cord

Lighting can significantly change the ambience of any room. In this room a soft natural glow was required and this was achieved by the use of a handmade lampshade, which offered both a delicate elegance and a gentle muted illumination. The basic shade can be enhanced by the use of a decorative fringe or ribbon, which can be sewn on to the edge of the skirt of the lampshade. The fabric chosen in this project was a pale fine-weave flame-retardant linen; it was gently gathered around the top of a lampshade frame and then pulled together with ribbon and allowed to hang in soft folds over the lamp base. Fringing completed the look. This lampshade is easy to make and will add a charming personal touch to any bedroom.

1 To calculate the amount of fabric needed for the lampshade, measure the circumference of the frame at the widest point then multiply this by two; this will give the width of fabric required. To calculate the length needed, measure the height of the lampshade frame. Then add 4¾in (12cm) to this to allow for turning and hemming at top and bottom.

2 Cut out the fabric with dressmaker's shears. Carefully fold over ¾in (2cm) of one long edge of the fabric and press with an iron. Then fold the edge over 2⅜in (6cm) and press again. Insert pins to secure the fold. Repeat this process at the opposite long edge of the fabric, but this time making the second fold only ¾in (2cm) deep.

3 Baste the two hems, then, using a sewing machine, stitch the hems ⅛in (3mm) from each inner edge. On the wider folded edge, measure ¾in (2cm) from the line of hem stitches and mark this along the whole width of fabric using tailor's chalk. Baste along this chalked line and then machine-stitch, finishing the threads off neatly at each end.

4 Lay the fabric flat so the hems are facing downward. Cut a length of pom-pom fringing to fit along the length of the lampshade. Pin this along the hemmed edge of the lampshade. Then baste and machine-stitch the fringe in place along the line of hem stitches.

5 Fold the fabric in half, right sides facing and raw edges together. Leaving a ½in (12mm) seam, stitch the sides together. Turn the shade right side out. Cut a slit in between the two lines of stitching in the top layer of fabric at the top of the shade. Using a tapestry needle, thread ribbon through the slit and along the channel, gathering the fabric as you go. Tie the ribbon ends.

6 Fit the lampshade frame inside the fabric shade and secure in position with large loop stitches sewn around the gathered fabric and the top wire ring of the frame. Then lift the shade and give it a gentle shake to settle the fabric in place. Stitch small looping stitches attaching the folds of fabric to the bottom ring of the frame. Attach the lampshade to the lamp base to finish.

Lavender sachets

MATERIALS

gauze

dressmaker's shears

sewing thread

sewing machine

dried lavender

paper

iron

pins

ribbon

button or bow

Lavender scent always conjures up images of long carefree summer holidays spent in the south of France where the days are trouble free and the nights warm and romantic. Aromatherapists and herbalists recognize the beneficial qualities that lavender has to offer when used as an essential oil; it is a natural sedative and has been used since time began to calm and soothe our nerves. The scent that it gives off evokes feelings of relaxation and peace, making it a perfect companion to a good night's sleep. This project shows how to create your own lavender sachets that you can hang on bedposts, mirror frames or drawer handles in the bedroom to fill the room with the soft perfume of lavender.

EXPERT TIPS

• *Use an open-weave fabric to make sachets. Make sure that the fabric is pressed with a hot iron prior to use. If you find it difficult to cut out and sew the fabric shape, place a thin layer of tissue between the gauze layers, which can then be removed prior to filling the bag.*

• *Use only dried lavender to fill sachets, as mold can occur if fresh lavender is used.*

1 Sachets are usually square, circular, or heart shaped. Carefully cut two matching shapes from a piece of gauze for each sachet. Here, two heart shapes are cut out.

2 Baste the two shapes together, then machine stitch around the shapes, about ¼in (6mm) from the edge, leaving the last few inches (centimeters) unsewn. Gently turn the sachet the right way out through the unstitched gap, teasing the fabric into the correct shape.

3 Fill the gauze sachet with dried lavender. To do this, make a small paper funnel, place the end of the funnel into the gauze pocket, then fill it with dried lavender and gently shake in the contents. Don't overfill the sachet as extra space allows the full fragrance of the lavender to be released.

4 Turn in the edges of the opening in the sachet and press gently with a hot iron. Pin, then baste the opening closed. Pressing the edges together, carefully sew the remaining edge by hand using small neat slipstitches. Then gently pull the heart sachet back into shape and shake it to disperse the contents evenly.

5 Attach a loop of ribbon to the center of the sachet with a few small stitches. Then stitch a button or bow on to the point where the ribbon is joined to the sachet; this will disguise any clumsy stitching and adds a dainty finishing touch.

MAKEOVER PROJECT

Matisse Style

With its decor of pink, green, turquoise, and yellow, this bedroom emits a sunny, happy atmosphere. An eclectic mix of colorful fabrics, ornaments, and flowering plants adds to the character in the room.

The inspiration for this room came from a painting entitled "The Open Window" by Henri Matisse, which is actually featured in the room, hanging above the bed. The effect of the painting is of a riot of color and pattern, and very bohemian in feel.

PROJECTS FROM THIS
MAKEOVER SHOW YOU

- HOW TO BLEND
  COLORS

- HOW TO PAINT A FRIEZE

- HOW TO STENCIL
  FABRIC

- HOW TO MAKE A
  CURTAINED SCREEN

In this makeover, a similar effect of color and space was sought. So, the walls were painted in turquoise and pink, with the wall texture built up by the use of several tones of color, applied using brushes of various sizes. The wooden floor was also distressed in a bright blue, while the window frame and door were painted in a rich bright yellow, with orange dragged over the top. The furniture was distressed with turquoise over a sea green base; the wrought-iron chair was chosen because it echoed the iron railings in the picture. The use of several colors is effective because the colors are all of the same tonal value.

PREPARATION

It may appear at first glance that the need for careful preparation for a room like this is unnecessary, as the finished look is quite rough. Nevertheless, the usual rules of decorating apply; the walls and ceiling still need to be checked and any cracks filled with all-purpose filler. The look was achieved by layering the paint, so the need for good adherent surfaces is paramount. To achieve this, rub down thoroughly all painted surfaces and prime them securely with water-based all-purpose primer. Mask off areas of different color before applying paint so that you get clean straight edges.

Choose the paint colors that you intend to use in your bedroom and, if you are unsure, paint a small test area on a bedroom wall to check that the colors work well together before starting.

BLENDING COLORS

Although the color of the wall surrounding the window may look pink, it is actually a combination of three different paint colors, which have been blended together using different sizes of brush. This method of blending color gives greater depth and interest to a surface and can be a useful way of lightening a dark area of wall without there being too much contrast. It is also useful if the walls to be painted are slightly chipped or pitted, as the nature of the paint effect is to produce an aged, distressed look.

EXPERT TIP
• *When using brush-strokes of color to build up a tone, it is important to maintain an overall view of the surface. Every now and then, step back and take a wider look. Try to work evenly across the whole area, blending as and where you need to. It is often easy to get carried away on one area. If this does occur, allow the area to dry and then apply the new paint quickly over the top, blending in the missing lighter or darker tones, until you have achieved an overall evenness to the surface.*

1 Using an all-purpose brush, apply a coat of medium pink latex paint over the surface. Brush it up and down to cover the surface evenly.

2 Using a smaller brush, apply pale orange latex paint over the pink, blending it carefully into the first coat. Using a smaller brush changes the scale of brushmark and the tone of color, which adds to the overall effect.

3 Using a large all-purpose brush, apply pale pink latex paint, blending the color roughly into the first two coats. The finished effect should be a mixture of the three different paint colors, while still allowing patches of each color to show.

Painting a frieze

MATERIALS

ruler

soft pencil

carpenter's level

artist's brush

latex paint: white, red, orange, green

varnish brush

clear water-based varnish

Paint can be used to create a huge range of visual effects. Even if you have never painted before, it is possible to paint a frieze on your wall. If your artistic skills are limited, you can copy an image from a book or magazine or, as here, from part of the Matisse painting. In this project, a shelf was placed beneath the image for an amusing touch. If you feel unhappy at the thought of copying freehand, there are processes you can use to translate your chosen image from book to wall. The first thing to do is to trace over the image using a pencil. Then draw a grid over the top. Next, number all the squares, and draw a grid directly on the wall to the size you intend to have your image. Number these squares so that they correspond to your original grid, then transfer your image square by square. Alternatively, if you have access to a slide projector, you can project and enlarge your image directly on to the wall.

1 Measure and mark the area of the wall where you intend to paint your image. Use a level to ensure that the marked line is straight. This will act as a guide when painting.

2 Using a soft pencil, begin to sketch the outlines of your chosen motif on the wall. This particular image consisted of three pots of flowering geraniums.

3 Starting with the lightest tones, begin to apply patches of latex paint over the penciled outlines. Do not paint neat brushstrokes; be bold and daub the paint on the wall. Aim for a random effect.

4 Add touches of orange and red paint to the frieze, applying it roughly to build up the design. The brushstrokes should simply suggest the flowers, rather than be accurate reproductions of actual petals.

5 Add daubs of green paint to suggest the leaves to complete your painted image. Allow to dry thoroughly, then brush a coat of clear varnish over the top to seal the frieze and protect it from any abrasions.

MATERIALS

photocopier

decorative images

tracing paper

pencil

stencil card

carbon paper

masking tape

black waterproof
marker pen

cutting mat

craft knife

waterproof varnish

fabric paint

artist's brushes

fabric

lining paper

stapler and staples

tape measure

low-tack masking tape

stippling brush

Stenciling fabric

The work of the artist Matisse has long influenced fabric and wallpaper designers. The wonderful use of color and design within Matisse's paintings positively oozes enthusiasm. In this project, you can learn how to print fabric with bright cheerful colors—orange, yellow, red, cobalt blue, and brilliant emerald green—to create your own bit of the south of France. This Matisse-inspired fabric can then be used as curtaining, as a bed cover, as a dressing table skirt, or made into cushions to brighten up any bedroom.

1 Photocopy two or three images from some of Matisse's paintings, enlarging them if desired. The shapes here were taken from two works: "The Sheaf" (1953) and "The Parakeet and the Mermaid" (1952). Trace around the photocopied images.

2 Place the carbon paper on top of the stencil card, and lay the tracing on top. Secure with masking tape. Go over the outlines with pencil to transfer the image. Then remove the tracing and carbon paper and go over the outlines on the stencil card with a thick black waterproof marker pen.

3 Place the stencil card on a cutting mat to protect the work surface. Then, using a sharp craft knife, carefully cut around the outside edge of the black line. Try to cut as smoothly as possible as ragged edges will not give a distinctive shape to the stencil. Discard the cutout piece of card.

4 Spray the stencil with waterproof varnish, allow to dry, then turn the stencil over and repeat. This will make the stencil stronger and will keep it from becoming soggy with the fabric paint.

5 Pour a small quantity of the two colors that you wish to mix into a resealable container (as you may need to store the color) and mix with a clean brush until integrated. Use the mixed color immediately; if the mix is left to stand, stir again just before using.

6 Stretch the fabric to be printed. This can be done easily over a pasting table. First, cover the pasting table with an old roll of lining paper. Then lay the fabric on top and staple the edges along both ends and a couple of times down the length, making sure that it is taut.

EXPERT TIP
• *If this is your first attempt at stenciling fabric do not be too ambitious in your choice of image—the simpler the better. It is easier to work with a limited color palette because it enables you to work more quickly and there is less risk of mistakes.*

7 Using a tape measure and a soft pencil, measure and mark on the fabric where you want your printed shapes to go. If you are intending to devise a repeating pattern, after marking where your shapes will go, you need to decide which color goes where. Lightly mark each square with the initials of the chosen color to prevent any confusion when the printing starts.

8 Place the stencil centrally over the designated square. Secure it on to the fabric with four small tabs of low-tack masking tape in the corners. Dip a stippling brush lightly into a pot of fabric paint and, starting in the middle of the stencil, stipple paint over the fabric, working slowly out to the edges. Do not overload the brush or paint will drip on to the fabric.

9 Repeat the same process with the second stencil, using a different color. Make sure you do not lean on the first painted stencil as you work, in case you smudge the paint.

10 Move on to the third stencil and stipple a third color of paint on to the fabric in the same way as in step 8. Carefully remove the stencils to reveal the stenciled images.

11 Measure the pattern with a tape measure, taking note of the distances between the various shapes. In this way you will be able to repeat the same layout along the fabric to make a repeating pattern.

12 Continue to stencil the fabric until it is covered. Then remove the stencils and allow the paint to dry. If there are any areas where the paint has leaked under the edges of the stencil, use a small soft pointed brush to paint over these, enlarging the shapes where necessary. If you wish to add any freehand detail to your painted fabric it can be done at this point.

EXPERT TIPS

• *Make sure that the fabric that you are printing on has the right absorbency for the fabric paint you intend to use. This can be tested by applying the paint to a swatch of the fabric and seeing the results. As a general rule, a natural-fiber fabric will be more receptive to fabric paint .*

• *Consider where you will use your newly stenciled fabric. If you want the fabric to be washable, you will need to use washproof paint. Always read the labels of fabric paint carefully before using.*

Making a curtained screen

A screen is a useful and practical accessory in a bedroom. It can be used to section off areas of a room discreetly, for instance to create a dressing area, or it can be used as a practical object on which to hang clothes. Alternatively, a screen can simply be an attractive item of furniture that adds a flamboyant touch to a room. Inspired by the way in which the screen in the Matisse room enabled several fabrics to be displayed, softening the room with both color and texture, this project takes a rather plain open screen, and transforms it into a wonderfully ornamental piece of furniture. Screen frames are available in varying forms, ranging from flat-packed kits to those already assembled. For the purposes of this project it is assumed that the screen frame has already been assembled.

1 Using an all-purpose paintbrush, paint the screen frame in your desired color of latex paint. Brush on the initial coat thinly as this will act as both a priming agent and a sealant. Allow to dry, then rub the frame down with fine-grit sandpaper. Apply a second coat.

2 Measure the height and width of each panel of the screen, adding 1½in (4cm) to each measurement to allow for hems. Cut out your chosen fabric accordingly. Turn over each long side of the fabric ½in (12mm) and press, then machine-stitch.

3 Fold over ½in (12mm) of the fabric at the short edges and press. Turn over a further 1¼in (3cm), baste, and machine-stitch. Pin and baste another line ½in (12mm) from the hem line and parallel to it on both top and bottom hems, then machine-stitch along this line.

4 Using an awl, make a small hole in the four corners of each of the screen panels. Screw a small screw eye into each hole. Cut lengths of curtain wire to fit between each pair of hooks.

5 Screw a small hanging hook into one end of a cut piece of curtain wire. Feed it through the stitched channel at the top of each curtain. Repeat to thread the bottom channel. Screw on a hook to the opposite end of each wire.

6 Attach each of the curtains to the screen panels by hooking the hanging hooks through the screw eyes at the top and bottom of each panel of the frame. Readjust the curtain gathers as necessary for an even finish.

Brushes

NATURAL-BRISTLE BLENDER/ SOFTENER BRUSH

A necessary expense for any serious decorative artist, this brush is made from very soft, long bristles of pure badger hair. Use it to tickle away brushstrokes from wet glazes and to give an out-of-focus appearance. It is essential for marbling work and useful in creating a color-washed effect. Meticulous cleaning is important as badger brushes are expensive to replace. Condition them with hair conditioner regularly.

ARTIST'S BRUSHES

Usually made from hog's hair and very stiff, artist's brushes are invaluable as detailing brushes and for mixing smaller quantities of paint. Cheap brushes are fine, unless you are using them for mural work, in which case better-quality brushes will give a more even brushstroke. The bristles of good-quality artist's brushes are slightly curved in toward the top of the brush, rather than being unnaturally straight.

FINE ARTIST'S BRUSHES

For detailing and fine mural work, a selection of medium-quality fine artist's brushes is important. Imitation sable or nylon work well and are less expensive than real sable or pony-hair brushes. Store them in a tube or brush wrap; do not store soft brushes in a pot with the bristles pointing downward as they will bend.

DUSTING BRUSH

This has endless uses, from dusting items before painting to dragging and color-washing. Natural bristle is more flexible and durable. Dusting brushes continue to perform well, even when they begin to wear into a stump.

DRAGGING BRUSH

This is a special brush with extra-long flexible bristles for creating a fine, striped effect. If you have a choice of dragging brush, always select one with a comfortable handle.

FLOGGER

This brush has extremely long, floppy bristles which, when gently tapped into wet glaze, create the distinctive flecks seen in natural wood grains such as oak.

VARNISHING BRUSH

Not essential but a joy to work with, a varnishing brush looks just like an all-purpose brush until you turn it to the side and see that it is only about ¼in (5mm) thick. The bristles are very flexible, hold a lot of varnish or paint, and help to feather oil-based paints in particular so that a perfectly smooth paint surface is obtained with minimum effort.

STIPPLING BRUSH

Use a stippling brush for removing brushstrokes and for creating a dotty, stippled paint effect. Most decorators use stippling brushes about 2in (5cm) square. Larger stipplers are faster to work with but become heavy as the hours pass. Stippling brushes are expensive and can be replaced in a pinch with a large paintbrush from which the loose bristles have been carefully picked out. If you use a paintbrush be sure to move it around as you work in order to avoid the imprint of the straight edges showing.

ALL-PURPOSE BRUSHES

A good selection of general all-purpose brushes is the starting point for any decorator. Buy the most expensive you can afford; cheap brushes will shed many hairs and not last long. When buying, press the bristles firmly to make sure there is no hole in the middle of the bristles that has been filled with a wooden wedge. This will fill with paint and the brush will drip.

WALLPAPER PASTING BRUSH

Use this large brush for smoothing wallpaper into position on a wall. It is wide and comfortable to handle for long periods at a time.

SASH BRUSHES

Originally designed to help with the painting of complicated sash windows, sash brushes are available with pointed or rounded tips. They are perfect for edging and lining, and also for stippling paint on small areas or when control is required. With a little practice you will be able to apply paint in a perfectly straight line by using a sash brush. It may well become an essential part of your decorating kit and reduce your masking tape expenses.

RADIATOR BRUSH

This is a standard all-purpose brush attached to a long-angled handle; it is helpful for painting behind radiators and pipework.

CHOOSING BRUSHES

• Good bristles have split ends, cheap nylon and bad bristles do not. It is easier to achieve a smooth finish with fine, soft bristles.

• Always use the narrowest brush you can bear as this will give you greater control and a longer period of time before a brush becomes too heavy.

Tools

ROLLERS

Use long-piled rollers for textured finishes or uneven surfaces and short-piled rollers for a smooth finish. A foam roller is useful for a smooth finish with oil-based paints but may bubble or "orange peel.: Work slowly with a well-loaded roller to avoid this. The small rollers sold for gloss paint are a useful addition to any painter's kit as they can be cleaned more easily than larger rollers.

SANDPAPER

Available in different grits, sandpaper is used for rubbing down and smoothing surfaces prior to painting, and for cleaning any drips of paint from a carpet.

ICE CUBE TRAY

Useful as a palette that holds a little sample of many colors at one time; it is easy to hold in one hand at the top of a ladder when painting detailing and murals.

MOHAIR PAINT APPLICATORS

These are wonderful speed painters, faster than a brush and smoother than a pile roller. Made from foam with a mohair painting surface, they are available in a wide range of sizes. These applicators are more economical with paint and much easier to wash than rollers. Work in every direction adjusting the pressure from light to heavy as the applicator runs out of paint.

TACK CLOTHS

These are sold as disposable cloths on a roll, or separately packed. They are lightly impregnated with spirits and oils and are perfect for wiping away dust after sanding a wooden item prior to priming, painting, and varnishing it. The oils and spirits can also help with cleaning paintwork prior to painting, but heavy-duty cleaner should be used if you are going to use a water-based paint.

TOOLS FOR GLAZE WORK

Not all glaze finishes require expensive, special brushes. Plastic bags can be wadded up and used to create a leathery effect, corks can be jabbed in to the glaze for a fossil effect, and rags used to create a soft, mottled look. Experiment with anything that will not leave lint or fluff in the glaze—try plastic wrap or foil and even the side of your fist or your fingertips.

PAINT TRAYS

Not just for rolling paint, these are also useful for holding open cans of paint and for mixing small quantities of paint.

DISPOSABLE PAPER PALETTE

Use this for tiny quantities of several colors at one time. The tear-off sheets eliminate any cleaning at the end of the day. Very comfortable to hold for long periods.

PAINT BUCKETS

Sturdy and reliable containers for a can of paint or a glaze mixture. A bucket can be hung from the top of a ladder with a meat hook or the handle. Keep an empty bucket handy for putting wet brushes in. Plastic buckets need not be washed after use and can be reused after the paint has dried until eventually you throw them away. Steel buckets are more expensive and therefore require more care and cleaning.

MAULSTICK

This is a cane with a soft ball of chamois leather or cloth tied to the end. For high work that requires a very steady hand, hold the maulstick in your nonpainting hand, supporting the cane under your arm. Rest the ball on the wall. You can then rest your painting wrist on the stick and remain steady, even for minute details. You can make a maulstick by attaching a cut tennis ball to one end of a can with a large square of chamois leather wrapped over the ball and tied securely to the cane.

Suppliers & Acknowledgments

The following companies supplied paints, wallpapers, furniture, and accessories:

Designers Guild
267–77 Kings Road
Chelsea
London SW3 5EN
Tel: 0171-351 5775
Wallpaper, cushions, teddy bear and jug used in lemon and lime room.

The publishers wish to thank the following photographers and organizations for their kind permission to reproduce the photographs in this book on the following pages:
page 6 (top) Jacques Dirand (Designer Michael Klein) / Interior Archive; page 6 (bottom) Tom Leighton / Homes and Gardens / Robert Harding; page 7 (top) Christopher Drake / Homes and Gardens / Robert Harding; page 7 (bottom) Simon Kenny / Belle / Arcaid; page 12 Tom Leighton / Homes and Gardens / Robert Harding; page 13 Paul Ryan (Designer Frances Halliday) / International Interiors; page 15 Simon Kenny / Belle / Arcaid.

Franklins
161 Camberwell Road
London SE5
Tel: 0171-703 6429
Antique French bed used in natural room and lemon and lime room

Habitat
Various branches
Tel: 01645 334433 for information
Various accessories

ICI Paints
Wexham Road
Slough
Berkshire SL2 5DS
Tel: 01753 550555
Paints

Ikea
Various branches
Tel: 0181-208 5600 for information
Bedside tables, slatted shoe rack, lantern, and rag rug used in Matisse room

Plough Homecraft Company
352-6 Lordship Lane
East Dulwich
London SE22 8LZ
Tel: 0181-693 4785
Decorator's materials

Index

DEDICATION

For my husband, Trevor, and my two children, Amber and Barnaby, without whom "I would be lost in space."

AUTHOR'S ACKNOWLEDGMENTS

Thanks to Tim Imrie and his team for their superb photography, hospitality, and for making our time in the studio such fun. Thanks also to Fanny for her amazing ability to find exactly the right thing and then know exactly where to put it. A big thank you to the two Sarahs, Sara Colledge for seeking me out and not giving up, and Sarah Duffin for her support and hard work, which was always done with a smile.

First published in North America
in 2001 by Betterway Books
an imprint of F&W Publications, Inc.
1507 Dana Avenue
Cincinnati, OH 45207
1-800/289-0963

Copyright © 1999 Murdoch Books (UK)

ISBN 1-55870-602-X

All rights reserved. No part of this book may be reproduced in any form or by any electronic or mechanical means including information storage and retrieval systems without permission in writing from the publisher, except by a reviewer, who may quote brief passages in a review.

Editor: Heather Dewhurst
Designers: Siân Keogh and Martin Laurie at Axis Design
Photographer: Tim Imrie
Stylist: Fanny Ward
Series concept and Creative Director: Marylouise Brammer
Commissioning Editor: Anna Sanderson
CEO & Publisher: Anne Wilson
International Sales Director: Mark Newman
Color separation by by Bright Arts in Hong Kong
Printed in Singapore by Tien Wah Press